VEHICLES
ON THE JOB

WATER VEHICLES

BY **JAMES BOW**

NORWOOD HOUSE PRESS

Cover: Container ships carry items all over the world.

Norwood House Press
P.O. Box 316598
Chicago, Illinois 60631

For information regarding Norwood House Press, please visit our website at:
www.norwoodhousepress.com or call 866-565-2900.

LIBRARY OF CONGRESS CATALOGING-IN-PUBLICATION DATA

Names: Bow, James, author.
Title: Water vehicles / by James Bow.
Description: Chicago, Illinois : Norwood House Press, [2018] | Series: Vehicles on
    the job | Includes bibliographical references and index.
Identifiers: LCCN 2018003250 (print) | LCCN 2018004755 (ebook) | ISBN
    9781684042302 (ebook) | ISBN 9781599539461 (hardcover : alk. paper)
Subjects: LCSH: Ships--Juvenile literature. | Boats and boating--Juvenile literature. |
    Submarines--Juvenile literature.
Classification: LCC VM150 (ebook) | LCC VM150 .B658 2018 (print) | DDC 623.82-
    -dc23
LC record available at https://lccn.loc.gov/2018003250

312N—072018
Manufactured in the United States of America in North Mankato, Minnesota.

CONTENTS

Note: Words that are **bolded** in the text are defined in the glossary.

A crew member carefully studies what she sees through the periscope.

CHAPTER 1

ACTION ABOVE AND BELOW THE WAVES

A **periscope** pops up above the waves. Below the waves, a submarine captain wants to know what is happening on the surface.

Small sailboats zip past. Big oil tankers float in the distance. Tiny, strong tugboats guide a giant container ship. A man in a rowboat puts away his oars and pulls out a fishing line.

Sometimes, the water is so crowded it seems the only way to get through it is to go under the waves. That's what the submarine was built to do.

Many different water vehicles can travel to a busy harbor.

PARTS OF A SUBMARINE

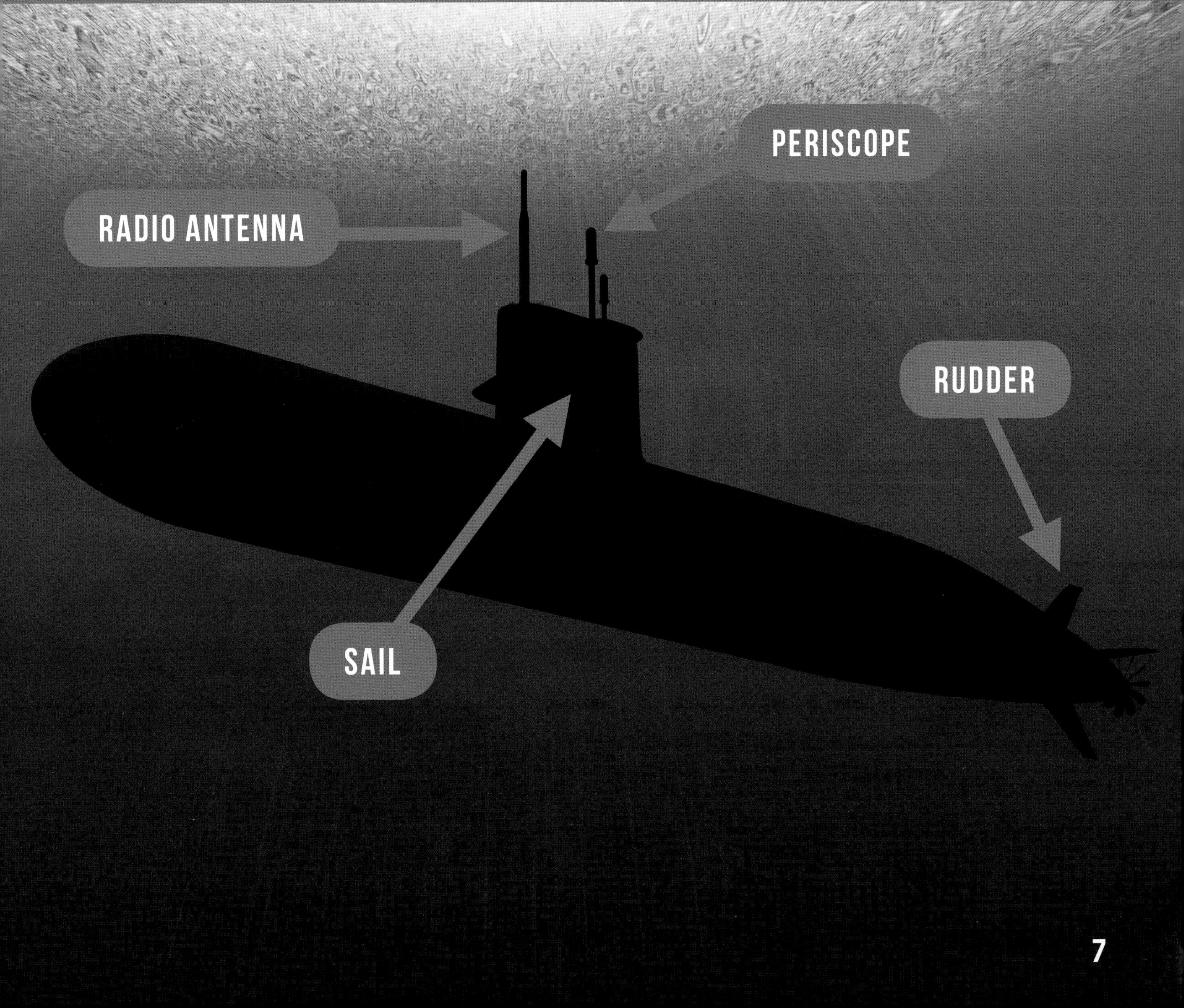

PERISCOPE

RADIO ANTENNA

RUDDER

SAIL

To trim the sails is to adjust them so they catch the wind properly.

CHAPTER 2

SAILBOATS

People have used sails to catch the wind and move their boats for thousands of years. Sails are big pieces of cloth. They catch the wind to move the boat. Sailors adjust the sails to sail with the wind or sail against it. Today, people mostly use sailboats for fun or racing.

Boats are often made of **fiberglass** and aluminum. Both materials are watertight, lightweight, and strong. The body of a boat is called the hull. Sails hang from masts. The front of a boat is called the bow. The back is called the stern. Facing the bow, the left side of the boat is called port, and the right is starboard. Near the center of the boat is one or more tall masts. The sails hang from the masts.

Modern sails are carefully made. Sailmakers consider how much a sail has to stretch to catch the wind and pull the boat. They have the plans chalked out on the floor of their workshop. This helps them cut the material to size. They sew in reinforcements, metal slides, and **grommets**. Sailors can count on their sails to work without ripping.

Some new sailboats are small. They might be just 11 feet (3.4 m) long. They can carry one or two sailors. Luxury boats can be bigger. They may have living quarters. The crew can sleep on board and take longer trips.

Different styles of sailboats rely on different sizes and shapes of sails to move through the water.

The Staten Island Ferry carries about 70,000 passengers per day between Staten Island and Manhattan in New York.

CHAPTER 3

POWERED BOATS

Many boats are powered by fuel such as **diesel**. Cruise ships are like floating hotels. **Yachts** and houseboats allow people to live on the water. They can move to different ports when they want. Ferries carry passengers and cars across water. They travel on lakes, rivers, and the sea.

People also use speedboats to race. The *Spirit of Australia* holds the record for fastest ship in the world. It reached 275.97 knots in 1978. That's more than 300 miles per hour (500 kph), which is faster than a high-speed train!

Ships are more than fun. They do important work. More than 4 million fishing vessels travel the oceans catching fish to sell. Other ships carry cargo in large shipping containers

The OOCL *Hong Kong* is one of the largest container ships. It is more than four football fields long!

STEM AT WORK: WHAT IS A KNOT?

It's more than how you tie your shoes! In boating, a knot refers to speed. One knot is the same as one nautical mile per hour. A nautical mile is about 1.2 regular miles (1.9 km).

Knots get their name from how sailors used to measure speed on boats. A special piece of wood would be tossed off the back of the boat. It was attached to a coil of rope with knots tied into it. As the ship moved, the wood floated behind it. It pulled the rope along with it. After a certain amount of time, sailors pulled in the rope. They counted how many knots had gone out. This told them the ship's speed in knots.

The world's largest container ships can carry more than 20,000 containers. They may not travel as fast as airplanes. But that's not the point. They can carry a lot more cargo than planes can. And this way costs much less.

There's work for smaller boats as well. Tugboats have plenty of power and can move through small spaces. They are used to push or pull big boats into port. Fire boats rush to help put out fires on ships or on the shore. Police boats make sure that everybody obeys the law on the water.

New technologies mean new ways of powering boats. Today's diesel-powered ships cause a lot of pollution. Solar technology is already using energy from the sun to charge batteries that power boats.

In May 2012, the MS *Tûranor PlanetSolar* became the first solar ship to travel around the globe.

The USS *Connecticut* submarine pushes up through ice while collecting data in the Arctic Ocean.

CHAPTER 4

BOATS UNDER THE SEA

While most boats ride the waves, submarines spend their time below them. Submarines explore places other boats can't go. They even explore beneath the polar ice caps!

Some submarines carry people on undersea tours. Passengers look out of windows at coral reefs and colorful fish.

ON THE JOB: SHIP CAPTAINS

Ship captains work with crews to set a ship's speed and course. Captains need to know where a ship is on the ocean to head in the right direction and avoid dangers. They need to know how boats work. They use geography, math, and science to do their jobs well. Finally, captains need to know how to help people on their ship work together.

Submarines control how deep they are by changing their **buoyancy**. **Ballast** tanks filled with air help them float on the surface. To sink, water fills those tanks and the air is pushed out. This makes the ship sink. To come back to the surface, the submarine releases air back into those tanks. This pushes out the water and the ship rises.

When a submarine goes underwater, no fresh air can get inside until it surfaces. The people inside the submarine breathe out carbon dioxide. This can be **toxic** when it builds up. Machines called scrubbers take the carbon dioxide out of the air. At the same time, oxygen tanks replace the oxygen. So do machines that make oxygen.

People around the world work, travel, and play on the water. Over 70 percent of Earth's surface is covered by water. With so much space to cross and explore, our water vehicles will always be on the job.

People who work on fishing boats use large nets to catch fish.

GLOSSARY

ballast (BA-luhst): A heavy material used to help control something or make it steady.

buoyancy (BOY-uhn-see): The ability to float on air or water.

diesel (DEE-zel): A special type of fuel used in some boat engines.

fiberglass (FIH-bur-glass): A material made from glass that is used to build boats.

grommets (GRAH-metts): Firm materials that protect the holes that ropes pass through.

periscope (PAIR-uh-skope): A device that uses mirrors and tubes to look around from behind something or beneath something.

toxic (TOCK-sik): Harmful to people, plants, or animals.

yachts (YAHTS): Boats used for racing or for living on.

FOR MORE INFORMATION

BOOKS

Bowman, Chris. *Monster Ships*. Minnetonka, MN: Bellwether, 2014. Discover different types of big ships from cruise ships to container ships.

Vamos, Samantha R. *Alphabet Boats*. Watertown, MA: Charlesbridge, 2018. Learn about different types of water vehicles from A to Z.

Willis, John. *Submarines*. New York, NY: Weigl, 2016. Explore submarines used by the military.

WEBSITES

Boat Safe Kids
www.boatsafe.com/kids/
A site for kids to learn how boating can be fun and safe, with homework helpers, questions and answers, and games.

Boats Afloat
www.pbskids.org/zoom/activities/sci/boatsafloat.html
Create a boat out of aluminum foil to learn how boats float.

INDEX

ABOUT THE AUTHOR

James Bow is the author of more than 40 educational books for children and young adults, a novelist, and a local columnist. He graduated from the University of Waterloo School of Urban and Regional Planning in 1991. Born in Toronto, he now lives in Kitchener, Ontario, Canada, with his author wife and his two daughters.